Yellowstone & Grand Teton National Parks 2024-2025

Budget-Savvy Tips for an Extraordinary Journey Through America's Majestic Wilderness

Kelly J. Cloutier

Disclaimer

The information in this book is provided as a general guide for travel planning purposes. While every effort has been made to ensure the accuracy and completeness of the information contained herein, the author and publisher assume no responsibility for errors, omissions, or changes in details, nor for any loss, injury, or inconvenience sustained by any person resulting from information or advice contained in this book.

Travel conditions, laws, and regulations are subject to change, and readers are advised to confirm such information with relevant authorities before making travel arrangements. Additionally, this guide includes recommendations for third-party services and providers, but the author and publisher do not endorse or assume any responsibility for these services or providers.

Readers are encouraged to exercise their own judgment and discretion when traveling and to take necessary precautions to ensure their personal safety and well-being.

Contents

Chapter 1: Introduction

Welcome to Your Adventure

Welcome to the ultimate journey through Yellowstone and Grand Teton National Parks! Nestled amidst the breathtaking landscapes of Wyoming, these two iconic parks offer a mesmerizing blend of natural wonders, wildlife encounters, and outdoor adventures. Whether you're a first-time visitor or a seasoned traveler seeking new thrills, this travel guide is your passport to discovering the magic of these pristine wilderness areas.

Imagine waking up to the crisp mountain air, surrounded by towering peaks, pristine lakes, and abundant wildlife. Yellowstone, America's first national park, is renowned for its geothermal wonders, including the iconic Old Faithful geyser and the colorful Grand Prismatic Spring. Grand Teton, with its jagged mountain ranges and serene alpine lakes, beckons hikers, climbers, and nature enthusiasts alike. Together, these parks form a haven for exploration and a sanctuary for those seeking solace in the great outdoors.

This guide is more than just a collection of tips and recommendations; it's an invitation to embark on a journey of discovery. Whether you're planning a family vacation, a solo adventure, or a romantic getaway, Yellowstone and Grand Teton offer something for everyone. From thrilling wildlife sightings to serene hiking trails and awe-inspiring scenic drives, the possibilities are endless.

Why Yellowstone and Grand Teton?

What makes Yellowstone and Grand Teton National Parks truly special? It's a question with myriad answers, each rooted in the parks' rich natural diversity and unparalleled beauty. Yellowstone, established in 1872, holds the distinction of being the world's first national park, a testament to its global significance. The park spans over 2 million acres, encompassing a diverse range of ecosystems, from vast meadows to dense forests and bubbling hot springs.

Yellowstone's geological wonders are a highlight for visitors. The park sits atop a volcanic hotspot, evident in its geothermal features such as geysers, hot springs, mud pots, and fumaroles. The iconic

Old Faithful, erupting regularly with impressive precision, captivates audiences year-round. Beyond its geological marvels, Yellowstone is also home to a remarkable array of wildlife, including grizzly bears, wolves, bison, elk, and more. Wildlife enthusiasts and photographers flock to the park for rare glimpses of these majestic creatures in their natural habitat.

Grand Teton National Park, located just south of Yellowstone, complements its neighbor with its striking mountain scenery and serene alpine lakes. The Teton Range, with its sharp peaks and glacial valleys, provides a stunning backdrop for outdoor adventures. Hiking trails wind through pristine forests and meadows, offering opportunities to spot wildlife and soak in panoramic vistas of the rugged landscape.

Together, Yellowstone and Grand Teton form a UNESCO World Heritage Site, recognized for their ecological importance and natural beauty. Beyond their physical attributes, these parks embody a spirit of conservation and stewardship, inviting visitors to connect with nature and appreciate the delicate balance of wilderness preservation.

How to Use This Guide

Navigating the wonders of Yellowstone and Grand Teton is made easier with this comprehensive travel guide. Here's how to make the most of it:

1. Planning Your Trip: Begin by setting your travel goals and determining the best time to visit based on seasonal highlights and weather patterns. Use the itinerary suggestions to create a personalized plan that suits your interests and preferences.

2. Budgeting for Your Trip: Estimate costs and discover money-saving tips to make your vacation budget-friendly. Find recommendations for affordable accommodations, dining options, and activities that won't break the bank.

3. *Essentials for Traveling:* Pack efficiently with our suggested packing lists and learn about essential travel gear and gadgets. Ensure your health and safety with practical tips and guidelines for sustainable travel practices.

4. *Entry and Visa Requirements:* Understand passport and visa requirements, as well as customs and immigration procedures. Learn about the importance of travel insurance and the documents you need to carry during your trip.

5. *Getting There and Around:* Explore transportation options, including tips for navigating the parks and choosing between guided tours and independent exploration. Discover road trip essentials and rental vehicle options for seamless travel.

6. *Cultural Experiences:* Immerse yourself in the rich history and heritage of Yellowstone and Grand Teton. Learn about local traditions, festivals, and opportunities to engage with Native American culture during your visit.

7. *Top Attractions and Activities:* Dive into detailed descriptions of must-see landmarks, outdoor adventures, family-friendly activities, and hidden gems waiting to be discovered in both parks.

8. *Tips for a Memorable Trip:* Capture stunning photographs with our photography tips, stay connected with practical advice, and make the most of your time with insider tips for navigating the parks and handling emergencies.

This guide is designed to enhance your travel experience by providing essential information and insider insights. Whether you're planning a short getaway or an extended vacation, let this guide be your companion as you explore the wonders of Yellowstone and Grand Teton National Parks.

Chapter 2: Planning Your Trip

Planning a trip to Yellowstone and Grand Teton National Parks involves setting clear goals, crafting a well-thought-out itinerary, and making informed decisions about accommodations and activities. Whether you're drawn to the geothermal wonders of Yellowstone or the majestic peaks of Grand Teton, careful planning ensures you make the most of your adventure in these iconic destinations.

Setting Your Travel Goals

Before embarking on your journey, it's crucial to define your travel goals. What are you hoping to experience and achieve during your time in Yellowstone and Grand Teton? Here are some common goals travelers often set:

Nature and Wildlife Exploration: Yellowstone and Grand Teton are renowned for their diverse ecosystems and abundant wildlife. If you're passionate about nature photography or wildlife watching, your goal might be to spot grizzly bears, wolves, bison, or elk in their natural habitats.

Outdoor Adventure: Hiking, backpacking, kayaking, and fishing are popular activities in these parks. Setting a goal to conquer a specific trail, summit a peak, or paddle a serene lake can add excitement and purpose to your trip.

Educational and Cultural Experience: Yellowstone and Grand Teton have rich histories and unique cultural landscapes. You might aim to learn about the geology of geysers, understand Native American heritage, or attend ranger-led programs to deepen your understanding of these national treasures.

Relaxation and Rejuvenation: If your goal is to unwind amidst stunning natural beauty, you might prioritize finding tranquil spots for meditation, scenic drives, or quiet moments by the lakeside.

Once you've identified your travel goals, you can tailor your itinerary and activities to align with these aspirations, ensuring a fulfilling and memorable journey.

Creating an Itinerary

Crafting a well-planned itinerary is essential for maximizing your time and experiences in Yellowstone and Grand Teton National Parks. Here's how to create an effective itinerary:

1. ***Research and Prioritize:*** Begin by researching the main attractions, activities, and points of interest in both parks. Make a list of must-see landmarks, such as Old Faithful in Yellowstone or Jenny Lake in Grand Teton, and prioritize them based on your interests and travel goals.

2. *Allocate Time:* Estimate the time needed to explore each attraction or participate in activities. Consider factors such as travel time between locations, hiking durations, and potential wait times for popular attractions.

3. *Balance Your Schedule:* Strike a balance between must-see sights and leisure time. Avoid overloading your itinerary with activities, as it can lead to exhaustion and diminish the enjoyment of spontaneous discoveries. Allow flexibility for unexpected opportunities or changes in weather conditions.

4. *Consider Seasonal Variations:* Depending on the season of your visit, certain activities or roads may be closed due to weather conditions.

Factor in seasonal variations when planning outdoor activities and check for any park alerts or advisories.

5. *Plan for Downtime:* Include breaks in your itinerary to rest, enjoy meals, and appreciate the natural surroundings. Downtime allows you to recharge and fully immerse yourself in the park's beauty.

6. *Use Resources:* Utilize park maps, visitor centers, and online resources to gather detailed information and plan logistics. Park websites often provide updated information on trail conditions, road closures, and ranger-led programs that can enhance your experience.

7. *Be Realistic:* While it's tempting to squeeze in as much as possible, be realistic about your energy levels and travel pace. Prioritize quality over quantity to fully appreciate the unique landscapes

and wildlife encounters Yellowstone and Grand
Teton offer.

Booking Accommodations and Activities

Securing accommodations and activities in advance
is crucial, especially during peak seasons when
demand is high. Here's how to navigate booking for
your trip:

Accommodations: Yellowstone and Grand Teton
offer a range of lodging options, from campgrounds
and rustic cabins to lodges and hotels. Determine
your preferred type of accommodation based on
comfort, location within the park, and budget.
Popular lodging options include Old Faithful Inn in
Yellowstone and Jackson Lake Lodge in Grand
Teton. Book accommodations well in advance, as
they can fill up quickly, particularly during summer
months.

Camping: If you prefer camping, reserve campsites through the park's official website or by calling the reservation hotline. Be aware of camping regulations, including bear safety protocols and leave-no-trace principles.

Activities: Many activities, such as guided tours, boat rentals, and horseback riding, require reservations, especially during peak seasons. Research activity options that align with your interests and book in advance to secure your spot. Consider ranger-led programs and educational tours to enhance your understanding of the parks' natural and cultural heritage.

Flexible Booking: While it's advisable to book key accommodations and activities ahead of time, maintain flexibility in your schedule. Weather conditions or unexpected closures may necessitate adjustments to your plans. Have alternative options or backup activities in mind to make the most of your visit.

By setting clear goals, crafting a thoughtful itinerary, and making timely bookings for accommodations and activities, you'll ensure a well-planned and rewarding journey through Yellowstone and Grand Teton National Parks. Whether you're seeking adventure, relaxation, or cultural enrichment, these parks promise an unforgettable experience in the heart of the American wilderness.

Chapter 3: When to Visit

Choosing the best time to visit Yellowstone and Grand Teton National Parks is crucial for optimizing your experience based on seasonal highlights, weather patterns, and wildlife viewing opportunities. Each season offers unique advantages, whether you're drawn to vibrant wildflowers, spectacular geothermal displays, or abundant wildlife sightings.

Seasonal Highlights

Spring (April to June):

Spring marks the awakening of nature in Yellowstone and Grand Teton. As temperatures rise and snow melts, the parks come alive with blooming wildflowers and rushing waterfalls. It's an ideal time for hiking and exploring, with fewer crowds compared to summer. Wildlife, including newborn animals, becomes more active as they emerge from winter dens. Be prepared for variable weather conditions, including occasional snowstorms in higher elevations.

Summer (July to August):

Summer is peak season for visitors, thanks to warm temperatures and extended daylight hours. All park facilities, visitor centers, and roads are typically open, allowing access to popular attractions like Old Faithful and Jenny Lake. Hiking trails are fully accessible, making it perfect for outdoor enthusiasts. However, expect larger crowds and make accommodations and activity reservations well in advance. Wildlife sightings are frequent, especially around dawn and dusk.

Fall (September to October):

Fall brings a breathtaking display of colors as the park's foliage transforms into hues of gold and crimson. The weather remains pleasant during the day, although temperatures can drop significantly at night. Fall is an excellent time for photography, with the landscapes bathed in autumnal hues and wildlife actively preparing for winter. Crowds begin to diminish after Labor Day, offering a quieter and more serene experience.

Winter (November to March):

Winter transforms Yellowstone and Grand Teton into a serene winter wonderland. While many park roads and facilities close during winter, select areas remain accessible for cross-country skiing, snowshoeing, and snowmobiling. The geothermal features, such as geysers and hot springs, take on a mystical appearance when surrounded by snow and ice. Wildlife sightings are rarer but can be spectacular, especially in Lamar Valley where bison and wolves are frequently seen. Winter visitors should be prepared for cold temperatures and snowy conditions, but the solitude and unique beauty of the parks in winter are unparalleled.

Weather Patterns

Understanding weather patterns is essential for planning activities and packing appropriately:

Summer: Daytime temperatures in summer typically range from 70°F to 80°F (21°C to 27°C) in Yellowstone and slightly cooler in higher elevations. Afternoon thunderstorms are common, especially in July and August. Nights can be cool, so bring layers to stay comfortable.

Fall: Days are generally mild with temperatures ranging from 50°F to 70°F (10°C to 21°C). Nights become cooler, often dropping below freezing in October. Be prepared for variable weather conditions, including occasional rain and snow showers.

Winter: Winter temperatures in Yellowstone and Grand Teton can be severe, with daytime highs averaging between 20°F to 30°F (-7°C to -1°C) and nighttime lows dipping well below freezing.

Snowfall is frequent, creating pristine landscapes but requiring winter gear and precautions for outdoor activities.

Spring: Early spring can still be chilly with daytime temperatures gradually warming up from 30°F to 50°F (-1°C to 10°C). Snowmelt increases water levels in rivers and waterfalls, adding to the scenic beauty of the parks.

Best Times for Wildlife Viewing

Wildlife viewing is a highlight of any visit to Yellowstone and Grand Teton. Each season offers unique opportunities to observe the park's diverse fauna:

Spring: Wildlife becomes more active as they emerge from winter hibernation or migration. Look for newborn animals, including bison calves and bear cubs. Grizzly bears are frequently spotted near open meadows searching for food after hibernation.

Summer: Early mornings and late evenings are prime times for wildlife viewing when animals are most active. Bison herds roam freely throughout Yellowstone, while elk and moose frequent the meadows and riversides. Birds, including bald eagles and ospreys, are also abundant.

Fall: As temperatures cool, wildlife prepares for winter by foraging more actively. Bull elk bugle during the rutting season, attracting visitors eager to witness their dramatic displays. Wolves are occasionally spotted in Lamar Valley, making fall a rewarding time for wildlife enthusiasts.

Winter: Wildlife sightings are less frequent but can be extraordinary. Bison gather near thermal areas where geothermal heat keeps the ground free of snow. Wolves and coyotes are more visible against the snowy backdrop, and bald eagles gather near open water bodies.

Choosing when to visit Yellowstone and Grand Teton depends on your interests and preferences. Whether you prefer the vibrant colors of fall, the tranquility of winter, or the lively activity of summer, each season offers a distinct and unforgettable experience in these iconic national parks.

Chapter 4: Budgeting for Your Trip

Planning a budget-friendly trip to Yellowstone and Grand Teton National Parks involves careful consideration of expenses, cost-saving strategies, and finding affordable options for accommodations, dining, and activities. By managing your budget effectively, you can enjoy a memorable vacation without breaking the bank.

Money-Saving Tips

- Travel Off-Peak: Consider visiting during shoulder seasons like spring or fall when accommodations are often cheaper, and crowds are thinner. Rates for flights and rental cars may also be more affordable during these times.

- Book Early: Secure accommodations and activities well in advance to take advantage of early booking discounts and ensure availability, especially during peak seasons.

- Flexible Travel Dates: Be flexible with your travel dates to capitalize on cheaper rates for flights, accommodations, and activities. Use flight comparison websites and flexible date search options to find the best deals.

- Pack Light: Avoid checked baggage fees by packing light and sticking to carry-on luggage. This not only saves money but also time at airports and reduces the risk of lost luggage.

- Cook Your Own Meals: If camping or staying in accommodations with kitchen facilities, prepare your meals rather than dining out for every meal. Visit local grocery stores for ingredients and pack picnic lunches for days spent exploring the parks.

- Use Public Transportation: Utilize public transportation options within and between cities to save on rental car costs and parking fees. Many national parks offer shuttle services that provide convenient access to popular attractions.

- National Park Pass: Consider purchasing an annual National Park Pass if you plan to visit multiple parks within a year. The pass grants access to over 2,000 federal recreation sites and can save money on entrance fees.

- Seek Free Activities: Take advantage of free ranger-led programs, nature walks, and educational talks offered by the parks. These activities provide valuable insights into the park's natural and cultural history without additional costs.

- Travel Rewards Programs: Use credit cards that offer travel rewards or cash back on purchases related to travel expenses such as flights, accommodations, and dining. Accumulated points or cash back can offset future travel costs.

- Pack Essentials: Bring reusable water bottles and snacks to avoid purchasing expensive drinks and snacks at tourist locations. Stay hydrated and fueled throughout your adventures without overspending.

Affordable Accommodations

- ***Campgrounds:*** Yellowstone and Grand Teton offer numerous campgrounds with basic amenities such as restrooms and picnic tables. Fees are lower compared to lodges and hotels, making camping an affordable option for budget-conscious travelers. Reserve campsites in advance, especially during peak seasons.

- **_Lodges and Cabins:_** Both parks feature lodges and cabins operated by the National Park Service or private companies. While generally more expensive than campgrounds, these accommodations provide comfort and convenience in scenic locations. Look for budget-friendly options or special offers, especially in shoulder seasons.

- **_Motels and Hotels Outside the Park:_** Consider staying in motels or budget hotels located outside the parks but within a reasonable driving distance. These accommodations often offer lower rates and may include amenities such as complimentary breakfast and Wi-Fi.

Hostels and Guesthouses: Look for hostels or guesthouses in nearby towns like Jackson, Wyoming, or West Yellowstone, Montana. These options provide shared or private rooms at affordable rates and are ideal for budget travelers seeking social interaction and local insights.

Vacation Rentals: Explore vacation rental websites for cabins, cottages, or apartments available for short-term stays near the parks. Renting a private residence can offer cost savings, especially for families or groups traveling together.

Dining on a Budget

Picnics and Packaged Meals: Purchase groceries from local markets or supermarkets and pack picnic lunches for days spent exploring the parks. Picnic areas are available throughout Yellowstone and Grand Teton, offering scenic spots to enjoy meals.

Cooking Facilities: Choose accommodations with kitchen facilities or access to communal kitchens. Prepare your meals using local ingredients to save money on dining expenses.

Local Diners and Cafés: Visit local diners, cafés, and casual restaurants in nearby towns for affordable meals. Look for daily specials or early bird discounts offered by restaurants catering to both locals and tourists.

Food Trucks and Street Food: Seek out food trucks or street vendors offering affordable and delicious meals. These mobile eateries often provide quick and convenient options for budget-conscious travelers.

Share Meals: Share large portions or opt for appetizers instead of full entrees when dining out. Splitting meals reduces costs while allowing you to sample a variety of dishes.

Finding Deals and Discounts

- Online Travel Agencies: Use online travel agencies (OTAs) to compare prices and find exclusive deals on flights, accommodations, and rental cars. Sign up for newsletters or alerts to receive notifications about discounted rates and special promotions.

- Hotel and Lodge Packages: Many lodges and hotels within and near the parks offer package deals that include accommodations, meals, and activities. These packages can provide significant savings compared to booking each component separately.

- Member Discounts: Check if you qualify for discounts through memberships such as AAA, AARP, or military affiliations. These memberships often offer reduced rates on accommodations, activities, and dining at participating locations.

- Last-Minute Deals: Take advantage of last-minute deals offered by hotels, lodges, and tour operators. Flexibility with travel dates can lead to substantial savings on accommodations and activities.

- Local Coupons and Visitor Guides: Pick up local coupons, visitor guides, or brochures upon arrival in the parks or nearby towns. These resources often contain discounts and special offers for restaurants, attractions, and outdoor activities.

- Group Discounts: Traveling with a group or family? Inquire about group discounts on accommodations, guided tours, and activities. Many providers offer reduced rates for larger groups, making it more economical to explore the parks together.

By implementing these budgeting strategies and seeking out affordable options for accommodations, dining, and activities, you can enjoy a memorable and cost-effective trip to Yellowstone and Grand Teton National Parks. With careful planning and resourcefulness, your adventure in these natural wonders will be both enriching and financially sustainable.

Chapter 5: Essentials for Traveling

When preparing for a trip to Yellowstone and Grand Teton National Parks, ensuring you have the right essentials can significantly enhance your comfort, safety, and overall experience. From packing lists tailored to the parks' diverse environments to selecting appropriate travel gear and prioritizing health and safety considerations, thoughtful preparation ensures you're well-equipped for adventure in these iconic destinations.

Packing Lists

Creating a comprehensive packing list ensures you have everything you need for your journey through Yellowstone and Grand Teton National Parks. Here's a breakdown of essential items to include:

1. Clothing:

- Layered Clothing: Pack lightweight, moisture-wicking base layers, insulating mid-layers, and waterproof outer layers to prepare for varying weather conditions.
- Hiking Boots or Shoes: Choose sturdy footwear with good traction for hiking trails and uneven terrain.
- Hat and Gloves: Protect yourself from sun exposure and cold temperatures, especially in higher elevations.

2. Outdoor Gear:

- Daypack: Carry a comfortable daypack for hiking essentials such as water, snacks, sunscreen, and a first aid kit.
- Water Bottle or Hydration System: Stay hydrated with a refillable water bottle or hydration pack, particularly during outdoor activities.
- Binoculars: Enhance wildlife viewing opportunities by bringing compact binoculars with you.

3. Travel Documents and Essentials:

- Valid ID and Passport: Ensure you have valid identification and any necessary travel documents if traveling internationally or through border areas.
- National Park Pass: Carry your National Park Pass if you've purchased one for entry into Yellowstone and Grand Teton.
- Maps and Guidebooks: Bring park maps, trail maps, and a comprehensive guidebook

to navigate the parks' landscapes and attractions.

4. Personal Care and Hygiene:

- Sunscreen and Lip Balm: Protect your skin and lips from sun exposure, even on cloudy days.
- Insect Repellent: Ward off mosquitoes and other insects, especially during summer months and near water bodies.
- Toiletries: Pack travel-sized toiletries, including soap, shampoo, toothpaste, and any prescription medications.

5. Safety and Emergency Supplies:

- First Aid Kit: Carry a compact first aid kit with essentials such as bandages, antiseptic wipes, pain relievers, and any necessary medications.
- Emergency Contacts: Have a list of emergency contacts, including park

emergency services and local medical facilities.

- Whistle and Flashlight: Include a whistle for signaling and a small flashlight or headlamp with extra batteries for navigating in low-light conditions.

6. Miscellaneous:

- Camera or Smartphone: Capture memorable moments and stunning landscapes with a camera or smartphone equipped with a durable case.
- Portable Charger: Keep your devices charged with a portable charger to ensure connectivity and access to digital resources.

Tailor your packing list based on the season of your visit and specific activities planned. Prioritize lightweight and multipurpose items to maximize space and comfort during your exploration of Yellowstone and Grand Teton National Parks.

Travel Gear and Gadgets

Selecting the right travel gear and gadgets enhances convenience, safety, and enjoyment during your trip to Yellowstone and Grand Teton National Parks. Consider these essential items:

1. Backpack or Daypack:

- Choose a comfortable backpack or daypack with padded straps and ample storage for hiking essentials, water, snacks, and personal items.

2. Hiking Gear:

- Hiking Boots or Shoes: Opt for durable, waterproof hiking boots or shoes with good ankle support and traction for navigating varied terrain.
- Trekking Poles: Enhance stability and reduce strain on joints with adjustable trekking poles, especially on challenging trails.

3. Navigation Tools:

- GPS Device or Smartphone: Use a GPS device or smartphone with offline maps and navigation apps to track routes and locate points of interest.
- Compass and Map: Carry a compass and printed maps as backup for navigation in areas with limited or no cell service.

4. Photography Equipment:

- Camera with Lenses: Bring a camera with interchangeable lenses or a compact camera capable of capturing wildlife, landscapes, and close-up shots.
- Tripod: Stabilize your camera for long exposures and group photos with a lightweight tripod suitable for outdoor conditions.

5. Safety and Emergency Equipment:

- Personal Locator Beacon (PLB): Consider carrying a PLB for remote hiking or backcountry exploration to alert emergency services in case of distress.
- Emergency Blanket: Pack a compact emergency blanket to provide warmth and protection from the elements in unexpected situations.

6. Communication and Connectivity:
- Portable Charger: Keep devices charged with a portable charger or solar charger to maintain communication and access digital resources.
- Two-Way Radios: Use two-way radios to stay connected with travel companions in areas with limited cell service or during outdoor activities.

7. Weather Protection:
- Waterproof Gear: Invest in waterproof or water-resistant clothing, backpack covers,

and dry bags to protect gear from rain and water splashes.

- Sun Protection: Wear a wide-brimmed hat, sunglasses with UV protection, and apply sunscreen regularly to shield against sun exposure.

Health and Safety Considerations

Prioritizing health and safety considerations ensures a safe and enjoyable experience while exploring Yellowstone and Grand Teton National Parks. Follow these guidelines:

1. Physical Preparation:

- Fitness Level: Assess your fitness level and choose activities and trails that match your physical abilities. Start a fitness regimen before your trip to build endurance and strength.

2. Altitude and Environmental Conditions:

- Altitude Adjustment: Yellowstone and Grand Teton encompass varying elevations, affecting oxygen levels and exertion. Allow time to acclimate if traveling from lower altitudes.
- Weather Awareness: Monitor weather forecasts and prepare for sudden changes in weather conditions, including thunderstorms, strong winds, and temperature fluctuations.

3. Hydration and Nutrition:

- Water Intake: Stay hydrated by drinking water regularly, especially during outdoor activities and in high-altitude environments where dehydration can occur quickly.
- Healthy Snacks: Pack nutritious snacks such as trail mix, energy bars, and fruits to maintain energy levels throughout the day.

4. Wildlife Safety:

- Respect Wildlife: Observe wildlife from a safe distance and avoid approaching or feeding animals. Use binoculars and zoom lenses for close-up views without disturbing natural behavior.

- Bear Safety: Familiarize yourself with bear safety protocols, including carrying bear spray, making noise while hiking, and storing food properly to prevent bear encounters.

5. Emergency Preparedness:

- Emergency Contacts: Carry a list of emergency contacts, including park emergency services, local medical facilities, and travel insurance providers.

- First Aid Kit: Pack a well-equipped first aid kit with supplies for treating minor injuries, cuts, insect bites, and altitude-related symptoms.

6. Leave No Trace Principles:

- Environmental Stewardshi: Practice Leave No Trace principles by minimizing your impact on natural surroundings. Pack out all trash, stay on designated trails, and respect park regulations.

7. Travel Insurance:

- Coverage: Consider purchasing travel insurance that includes medical coverage, trip cancellation/interruption, and emergency evacuation to protect against unforeseen circumstances.

By preparing adequately with packing essentials, selecting appropriate travel gear and gadgets, and prioritizing health and safety considerations, you'll be well-prepared to embark on a memorable and safe adventure through Yellowstone and Grand Teton National Parks. Enjoy the breathtaking landscapes, diverse wildlife, and unparalleled outdoor experiences while exploring these natural wonders responsibly.

Chapter 6: Entry and Visa Requirements

Planning your visit to Yellowstone and Grand Teton National Parks involves understanding entry and visa requirements, customs and immigration procedures, as well as ensuring you have essential documents for a hassle-free journey. Whether you're traveling domestically within the United States or internationally, proper preparation ensures smooth entry into the parks and compliance with regulatory guidelines.

Passport and Visa Information

Domestic Travel (Within the United States):
If you are a U.S. citizen or resident traveling within the United States to Yellowstone and Grand Teton National Parks, you do not need a passport or visa.

A valid government-issued photo ID, such as a driver's license or state ID card, suffices for identification purposes at park entrances and during interactions with park rangers.

International Travelers:

For international travelers visiting Yellowstone and Grand Teton National Parks, entry requirements vary depending on your country of citizenship. Here are key considerations:

1. Passport: All international visitors must possess a valid passport. Ensure your passport is valid for at least six months beyond your intended stay in the United States.

2. Visa Requirements: Determine if you need a visa to enter the United States based on your nationality. Visa requirements vary, and it's essential to check with the nearest U.S. embassy or consulate well in advance of your travel dates.

3. _Visa Waiver Program (VWP):_ Citizens of certain countries may be eligible to travel to the United States for tourism or business purposes without a visa under the Visa Waiver Program. Travelers must apply for an Electronic System for Travel Authorization (ESTA) through the official U.S. Customs and Border Protection website before departure.

4. _B-2 Tourist Visa:_ If you do not qualify for the Visa Waiver Program, you may need to apply for a B-2 tourist visa at a U.S. embassy or consulate in your home country. This visa allows for leisure travel, including visits to national parks like Yellowstone and Grand Teton.

5. _Entry Requirement:_ Upon arrival in the United States, present your passport, visa (if applicable), and completed Customs Declaration Form (Form 6059B) to immigration officials at the port of entry. Be prepared to provide information about your travel itinerary and accommodation details.

6. *Transit Travel:* If you are transiting through a U.S. airport on your way to another destination, check if you need a transit visa based on your nationality and itinerary.

7. *Travel Restrictions and Update:* Stay informed about any travel restrictions, entry requirements, and updates related to COVID-19 or other public health concerns that may impact international travel to the United States.

Customs and Immigration Procedures

Navigating customs and immigration procedures is an integral part of international travel to Yellowstone and Grand Teton National Parks. Here's what to expect upon arrival:

1. Customs Declaration Form: Complete the Customs Declaration Form (Form 6059B) distributed onboard your flight or available at the port of entry. Declare all items purchased abroad, including gifts, food, and souvenirs, to customs officials.

2. Immigration Inspection: Upon disembarking from your flight or arriving at a U.S. port of entry, proceed to immigration inspection. Present your passport, visa (if applicable), and completed Customs Declaration Form to immigration officers.

3. Biometric Data Collection: Some travelers may undergo biometric data collection, such as fingerprints and facial recognition, as part of U.S. entry procedures.

4. Baggage Claim and Inspection: Retrieve your checked luggage from the baggage claim area and proceed to customs inspection. Customs officers may randomly select bags for inspection to ensure compliance with U.S. regulations.

5. _Prohibited Items:_ Familiarize yourself with prohibited and restricted items when entering the United States. Avoid carrying agricultural products, firearms, certain medications, and illegal substances, as they may result in fines or confiscation.

6. _Global Entry Program:_ Eligible travelers may expedite customs and immigration clearance through the Global Entry program, which requires pre-approval and a background check. Participants can use automated kiosks for faster entry into the United States.

7. _Customs Duties and Taxes:_ Be aware of customs duties and taxes applicable to goods exceeding personal exemptions. Consult the U.S.

Customs and Border Protection website or inquire with customs officials for specific guidelines.

Important Documents to Carry

Ensure you have essential documents readily accessible throughout your journey to Yellowstone and Grand Teton National Parks:

1. Passport: Carry your original passport with at least six months' validity beyond your intended stay in the United States.

2. Visa (if applicable): Keep a copy of your visa approval notice or visa stamp in your travel documents.

3. ESTA Approval (if applicable): Print or electronically save your ESTA approval confirmation for presentation upon arrival in the United States.

4. *Customs Declaration Form:* Complete and sign the Customs Declaration Form (Form 6059B) before arrival in the United States.

5. *Travel Itinerary:* Maintain a copy of your travel itinerary, including flight details, accommodation reservations, and transportation arrangements.

6. *Health Insurance Card:* Carry proof of health insurance coverage valid in the United States. Travel insurance that includes medical coverage and emergency evacuation is highly recommended.

7. *Emergency Contacts:* Carry a list of emergency contacts, including embassy or consulate information, travel insurance providers, and local emergency services.

8. Driver's License or ID Card: If you're a U.S. citizen or resident, carry a valid driver's license or state-issued ID card for identification purposes.

9. Credit Cards and Cash: Carry sufficient funds in U.S. currency or major credit cards for expenses such as dining, transportation, and souvenirs.

10. Park Passes: If you've purchased a National Park Pass or other entry permits for Yellowstone and Grand Teton National Parks, keep them easily accessible for verification at park entrances.

By understanding and fulfilling entry and visa requirements, adhering to customs and immigration procedures, and carrying essential documents, you'll ensure a seamless and compliant journey to Yellowstone and Grand Teton National Parks. Prepare in advance, stay informed about travel updates, and enjoy exploring these natural wonders responsibly and comfortably.

Chapter 7: Getting There and Around

Exploring Yellowstone and Grand Teton National Parks involves navigating vast landscapes and diverse ecosystems. Understanding transportation options, navigating park routes, and renting vehicles ensures you can efficiently explore these iconic destinations while maximizing your experience.

Transportation Options

1. Air Travel:

- Nearest Airports: The closest major airports to Yellowstone and Grand Teton are Jackson Hole Airport (JAC) near Jackson, Wyoming, and Bozeman Yellowstone International Airport (BZN) near Bozeman, Montana.

These airports offer domestic flights and limited international connections.

- Ground Transportation: Shuttle services, rental cars, and taxis are available from airports to nearby towns and park entrances. Plan your ground transportation in advance, especially during peak seasons.

2. Road Trips:

- Driving Distances: Yellowstone and Grand Teton are accessible by car from various U.S. cities, including Salt Lake City, Utah; Denver, Colorado; and Seattle, Washington. Consider embarking on a scenic road trip through neighboring states to reach the parks.

- Scenic Routes: Enjoy picturesque drives along designated scenic byways such as the Grand Loop Road in Yellowstone and the Teton Park Road in Grand Teton. Stop at viewpoints and pullouts to admire panoramic views of mountain ranges and wildlife habitats.

3. Public Transportation:

- Park Shuttles: Yellowstone offers a seasonal park shuttle system that operates between key attractions and visitor centers. The shuttles provide a convenient and eco-friendly way to explore the park without the hassle of driving.
- Local Buses: Some gateway towns, such as Jackson, Wyoming, offer local bus services to and from nearby attractions, including Grand Teton National Park.

4. Rail Travel:

- Amtrak: Amtrak's California Zephyr route stops in towns near Yellowstone and Grand Teton, including Salt Lake City, Utah, and West Yellowstone, Montana. Consider combining rail travel with local transportation options for a comprehensive park visit.

Navigating the Parks

1. Park Maps and Information:

- Visitor Centers: Begin your journey at park visitor centers to obtain maps, park newspapers, and information about current conditions, ranger-led programs, and points of interest.
- Park Maps: Carry detailed park maps highlighting scenic drives, hiking trails, picnic areas, and facilities. Maps are available at visitor centers and online through the National Park Service website.

2. Driving Tips:

- Speed Limits: Adhere to posted speed limits within the parks to ensure safety and wildlife protection. Reduced speed limits are enforced in wildlife-rich areas to minimize the risk of collisions.

- Traffic Conditions: Expect congestion and delays, especially during peak visitation periods and wildlife viewing opportunities. Plan for additional travel time to reach popular attractions and parking areas.

3. Hiking and Biking Trails:

- Trailheads: Access hiking and biking trails from designated trailheads located throughout Yellowstone and Grand Teton. Check trail conditions, elevation gain, and difficulty ratings before embarking on outdoor adventures.

- Trail Etiquette: Practice Leave No Trace principles by staying on designated trails, yielding to wildlife, and packing out all trash. Respect trail closures and wildlife management areas for conservation purposes.

4. Wildlife Viewing:

- Safety Precautions: Observe wildlife from a safe distance to avoid disturbing natural behaviors and potential hazards. Use binoculars and telephoto lenses for close-up views without approaching animals.
- Wildlife Jams: Be prepared for wildlife jams caused by animal sightings along roadways. Park in designated pullouts and use caution when photographing or observing wildlife near roads.

Renting Vehicles and Road Tips

1. Rental Vehicles:

- Types of Vehicles: Rent a compact car, SUV, or camper van suitable for navigating park roads and accessing trailheads. Reserve vehicles in advance, especially during peak seasons, to secure availability and competitive rates.

- Insurance Coverage: Review rental insurance options and coverage details to protect against damages, accidents, and theft during your park visit.

2. Driving Tips:

- Road Conditions: Yellowstone and Grand Teton feature paved roads, gravel roads, and scenic byways with varying conditions. Drive cautiously, especially on winding mountain roads and in inclement weather.
- Weather Preparedness: Monitor weather forecasts and road conditions before driving through the parks. Be prepared for sudden changes in weather, including snowstorms and high winds, particularly at higher elevations.

3. Parking and Facilities:

- Parking Areas: Utilize designated parking areas at visitor centers, trailheads, and attractions to ensure vehicle security and compliance with park regulations.
- Restrooms and Services: Plan rest breaks at park facilities equipped with restrooms, picnic areas, and information kiosks. Carry snacks, water, and essential supplies for day trips into remote areas.

4. Fuel Availability:

- Gas Stations: Locate gas stations within and near the parks to refuel vehicles before embarking on extended drives or backcountry adventures. Carry extra fuel if traveling to remote areas with limited services.

5. Road Closures and Alerts:

- Park Websites: Check park websites and social media channels for real-time updates on road closures, construction projects, and seasonal alerts affecting travel routes and park access.

- Alternative Routes: Identify alternative routes and detours to bypass closed roads or congested areas, ensuring continuity of your travel itinerary within Yellowstone and Grand Teton National Parks.

By familiarizing yourself with transportation options, navigating park routes, and renting vehicles equipped for park exploration, you'll optimize your journey through Yellowstone and Grand Teton National Parks. Embrace the scenic beauty, wildlife encounters, and outdoor adventures while adhering to park regulations and safety guidelines for a memorable park visit.

Chapter 8: Cultural Experiences

Exploring Yellowstone and Grand Teton National Parks goes beyond breathtaking landscapes and wildlife encounters; it offers a rich tapestry of cultural experiences deeply rooted in history, heritage, local traditions, and Native American cultures. Immerse yourself in the stories, traditions, and vibrant cultural tapestries that shape these iconic destinations.

History and Heritage of the Parks

1. Yellowstone National Park:

- Establishment: Established in 1872, Yellowstone is the world's first national park, renowned for its geothermal wonders, including Old Faithful geyser and the Grand Prismatic Spring.

- Conservation Legacy: Recognized as a UNESCO World Heritage Site, Yellowstone preserves diverse ecosystems, endangered species, and geologic marvels that captivate millions of visitors annually.
- Historic Lodges: Visit historic lodges such as Old Faithful Inn and Lake Yellowstone Hotel, showcasing rustic architecture and timeless charm amid natural surroundings.

2. *Grand Teton National Park:*

- Scenic Beauty: Grand Teton is celebrated for its towering mountain peaks, pristine lakes, and abundant wildlife, offering outdoor enthusiasts opportunities for hiking, mountaineering, and wildlife viewing.
- Homesteading and Settlement: Discover the park's human history through preserved homesteads, ranches, and pioneer cabins

that reflect early settlement and ranching traditions in the Jackson Hole Valley.

- Jackson Hole Museum: Explore exhibits at the Jackson Hole Museum in Jackson, Wyoming, highlighting local history, Native American artifacts, and pioneer life in the region.

3. *Shared History and Conservation Efforts:*

- Yellowstone-Grand Teton Connection: Learn about the interconnected history and conservation efforts between Yellowstone and Grand Teton National Parks, emphasizing wildlife corridors and ecosystem preservation.
- Fire Management: Understand the role of controlled burns and fire management practices in maintaining healthy forest ecosystems and promoting biodiversity within the parks.

Local Traditions and Festivals

1. Yellowstone Area:

- Old West Culture: Experience the spirit of the Old West through cowboy poetry gatherings, rodeos, and western-themed events in towns such as Cody, Wyoming, and West Yellowstone, Montana.

- Yellowstone Ski Festival: Attend the Yellowstone Ski Festival held annually in West Yellowstone, featuring cross-country ski races, clinics, and community events celebrating winter sports and outdoor recreation.

2. Jackson, Wyoming (Gateway to Grand Teton):

- Jackson Hole Rodeo: Witness the excitement of professional rodeo events at the Jackson Hole Rodeo, held weekly during the summer months, showcasing bull riding, barrel racing, and roping competitions.

- Fall Arts Festival: Participate in the Jackson Hole Fall Arts Festival, highlighting local and regional artistry through gallery exhibits, art auctions, and live demonstrations throughout the town.

3. Native American Powwows and Cultural Events:

- Eastern Shoshone and Northern Arapaho Tribes: Engage with Native American communities through powwows, cultural demonstrations, and storytelling sessions that celebrate traditions, music, and dance.
- Wind River Reservation: Visit the Wind River Reservation near Grand Teton, home to the Eastern Shoshone and Northern Arapaho tribes, to learn about tribal histories, languages, and contemporary issues.

Engaging with Native American Culture

1. Tribal Histories and Traditions:

- Shoshone and Arapaho Cultures: Discover the cultural heritage of the Eastern Shoshone and Northern Arapaho tribes, whose ancestral lands encompass present-day Wyoming and neighboring regions.

- Tipi Encampments: Experience traditional tipi encampments and learn about seasonal activities, storytelling, and ceremonial practices that reflect spiritual connections to the land.

2. Art and Craftsmanship:

- Beadwork and Textiles: Appreciate the artistry of Native American beadwork, textiles, and traditional crafts showcased in local galleries, museums, and cultural centers.
- Handcrafted Goods: Purchase authentic handcrafted goods such as jewelry, pottery, and woven baskets from Native American artisans at local markets and powwows supporting cultural preservation efforts.

3. Cultural Interpretation Programs:

- Interpretive Centers: Visit interpretive centers and heritage sites within Yellowstone and Grand Teton National Parks offering educational programs, exhibits, and guided tours highlighting Native American histories and cultural contributions.

- Ranger-Led Talks: Attend ranger-led talks and workshops focused on Native American perspectives on land stewardship, conservation practices, and environmental sustainability.

4. Respect and Cultural Sensitivity:

- Cultural Etiquette: Respect tribal protocols and traditions when interacting with Native American communities, including asking permission before photographing individuals or participating in ceremonial activities.
- Educational Resources: Access educational resources and publications provided by tribal councils, cultural organizations, and national park services to deepen understanding and appreciation of Native American cultures.

Preservation and Legacy

1. Environmental Stewardship:

- Collaborative Conservation: Support collaborative efforts between national park services, tribal governments, and conservation organizations to preserve cultural landscapes, wildlife habitats, and natural resources for future generations.
- Educational Outreach: Engage in educational outreach programs focused on cultural heritage, environmental stewardship, and sustainable tourism practices within Yellowstone and Grand Teton National Parks.

2. Community Partnerships:

- Cultural Exchanges: Foster cultural exchanges and partnerships that promote cross-cultural understanding, mutual respect, and shared responsibilities in preserving cultural diversity and natural heritage.
- Visitor Contributions: Contribute to local initiatives and nonprofit organizations

dedicated to supporting Native American communities, cultural revitalization projects, and youth education programs within the park regions.

Embrace the depth and diversity of cultural experiences awaiting you in Yellowstone and Grand Teton National Parks. From exploring historic sites and attending local festivals to engaging with Native American traditions and supporting cultural preservation efforts, each encounter enriches your journey through these treasured landscapes. Celebrate the legacy of conservation, heritage, and community stewardship embedded in the heart of these iconic national parks.

Chapter 9: Top Attractions and Activities

Exploring Yellowstone and Grand Teton National Parks unveils a world of natural wonders, outdoor adventures, and family-friendly activities. From iconic landmarks and geological marvels to thrilling outdoor pursuits and educational experiences, each attraction promises unforgettable moments amidst breathtaking landscapes.

Must-See Landmarks

1. Yellowstone National Park:

- Old Faithful Geyser: Witness the iconic eruption of Old Faithful, one of the most predictable geysers in the world, reaching heights of up to 180 feet.

- Grand Canyon of the Yellowstone: Marvel at the dramatic Lower Falls and vibrant canyon colors along viewpoints accessible via North Rim Drive and South Rim Drive.

- Mammoth Hot Springs: Explore terraces of travertine formations shaped by hot springs, showcasing intricate patterns and vibrant mineral deposits.

2. Grand Teton National Park:

- Grand Teton Range: Admire the majestic peaks of the Teton Range, including Grand Teton, Middle Teton, and Mount Owen, offering panoramic views from scenic overlooks and hiking trails.

- Jackson Lake: Enjoy water activities such as kayaking, paddleboarding, and scenic boat cruises on Jackson Lake, surrounded by mountain vistas and abundant wildlife.

- Mormon Row Historic District: Photograph historic homesteads framed by the Teton Range, capturing iconic barns and rustic structures dating back to early 20th-century settlement.

3. Shared Attractions:

- Yellowstone Lake: Discover the serene beauty of Yellowstone Lake, spanning 136 square miles and offering opportunities for fishing, boating, and lakeside picnics.
- Wildlife Viewing: Encounter diverse wildlife species, including bison herds, elk, moose, grizzly bears, and wolves, roaming natural habitats throughout both parks.
- Grand Prismatic Spring: Visit Yellowstone's largest hot spring, renowned for its vivid colors and microbial mats visible from the boardwalks of the Midway Geyser Basin.

Outdoor Adventures

1. Hiking and Backpacking:

- Yellowstone: Explore over 900 miles of hiking trails, ranging from easy walks to challenging backcountry routes, including trails to Mystic Falls, Avalanche Peak, and the Yellowstone River Picnic Area.
- Grand Teton: Embark on hikes such as Cascade Canyon Trail, Taggart Lake Loop, and the challenging trek to the summit of Grand Teton, rewarding adventurers with stunning alpine scenery.

2. Wildlife Watching:

- Safari Tours: Join guided wildlife safari tours or self-drive along wildlife-rich routes like Lamar Valley in Yellowstone, known for wolf packs, bison herds, and pronghorn antelope.
- Photography: Capture wildlife in their natural habitats during sunrise and sunset

hours, utilizing telephoto lenses and binoculars for close-up views of elusive species.

3. Water Activities:

- Kayaking and Canoeing: Paddle along scenic rivers and lakes, including Snake River in Grand Teton and Yellowstone River in Yellowstone, enjoying tranquil waters and panoramic vistas.
- Fishing: Cast a line for native cutthroat trout and other fish species in designated fishing spots throughout both parks, adhering to fishing regulations and obtaining necessary permits.

4. Winter Sports:

- Cross-Country Skiing: Explore groomed trails and backcountry routes for cross-country skiing and snowshoeing, with winter landscapes transforming Yellowstone and Grand Teton into snowy wonderlands.

- Snowmobiling: Navigate designated snowmobile trails in Yellowstone, accessing remote geothermal areas and winter wildlife habitats under the supervision of authorized outfitters.

Family-Friendly Activities

1. Junior Ranger Program:
- Educational Activities: Engage children in the Junior Ranger Program, offering educational activities, nature hikes, and interactive exhibits focused on wildlife conservation and park stewardship.
- Badge Ceremony: Attend Junior Ranger badge ceremonies held at visitor centers, where young participants pledge to protect national parks and receive badges recognizing their achievements.

2. Scenic Drives:

- Yellowstone: Drive along the Grand Loop Road, stopping at viewpoints such as Artist Point, Fountain Paint Pot, and Norris Geyser Basin to admire geothermal features and geological formations.
- Grand Teton: Explore Teton Park Road and Moose-Wilson Road, with opportunities for wildlife spotting, picnicking, and short walks to scenic overlooks accessible for all ages.

3. Ranger-Led Programs:
- Interactive Talks: Attend ranger-led programs featuring interactive talks, guided walks, and evening campfire programs discussing park history, wildlife ecology, and geological processes.
- Night Sky Programs: Join stargazing sessions and astronomy programs to observe celestial phenomena, constellations, and meteor showers against the backdrop of pristine night skies in the parks.

4. Visitor Centers and Museums:

- Educational Exhibits: Visit visitor centers and museums showcasing exhibits on park ecosystems, geology, Native American cultures, and early explorers who shaped the parks' histories.

- Interactive Displays: Explore hands-on displays and multimedia presentations offering insights into natural wonders, conservation efforts, and environmental challenges faced by national parks.

Conservation and Education

1. Environmental Stewardship:

- Leave No Trace Principles: Practice Leave No Trace principles by minimizing impact on natural habitats, packing out trash, and respecting wildlife habitats during outdoor activities.

- Conservation Initiatives: Support conservation initiatives through volunteer programs, citizen science projects, and fundraising efforts benefiting Yellowstone and Grand Teton National Parks.

2. Educational Outreach:

- School Programs: Participate in school group programs and educational field trips organized by park rangers, focusing on environmental science, outdoor recreation, and wilderness preservation.
- Youth Engagement: Inspire young learners through youth camps, nature workshops, and educational resources promoting outdoor exploration, wildlife observation, and ecological awareness.

3. Community Partnerships:

- Collaborative Efforts: Collaborate with local communities, nonprofit organizations, and academic institutions to promote sustainable tourism practices, cultural diversity, and community engagement within the park regions.

- Visitor Contributions: Contribute to park conservation funds, research grants, and educational scholarships supporting initiatives that protect natural resources and enhance visitor experiences in Yellowstone and Grand Teton National Parks.

Embrace the diversity of attractions and activities awaiting you in Yellowstone and Grand Teton National Parks, from iconic landmarks and outdoor adventures to family-friendly activities fostering a deeper connection with nature and cultural heritage. Explore, discover, and cherish the wonders of these pristine wilderness areas while preserving their ecological integrity for future generations to enjoy.

Chapter 10: Accommodation Guide

Luxury Hotels

1. Old Faithful Inn

- Price: $400-$800 per night
- Location: 3200 Old Faithful Inn Rd, Yellowstone National Park, WY 82190
- Booking Contact: +1 307-344-7311

The Old Faithful Inn, a historic hotel built in 1904, offers a unique lodging experience with its rustic charm and prime location adjacent to the Old Faithful geyser. The hotel features a range of accommodations from simple rooms to spacious suites. Its central location makes it an ideal base for exploring Yellowstone National Park.

2. Jackson Lake Lodge

- Price: $300-$700 per night
- Location: 101 Jackson Lake Lodge Rd, Moran, WY 83013
- Booking Contact: +1 307-543-3100

Located within Grand Teton National Park, Jackson Lake Lodge provides stunning views of the Teton Range and Jackson Lake. This luxurious lodge offers various amenities, including a heated outdoor pool, on-site dining options, and guided tours. The lodge's modern rooms and suites are designed to offer comfort and elegance amidst the wilderness.

3. Amangani

- Price: $1,200-$3,500 per night
- Location: 1535 NE Butte Rd, Jackson, WY 83001
- Booking Contact: +1 307-734-7333

Amangani, a top-tier luxury resort, is situated on the edge of a high mountain valley in Jackson. This exclusive resort boasts spacious suites with breathtaking views, a world-class spa, fine dining, and a heated outdoor infinity pool. The elegant design and impeccable service make Amangani a perfect choice for a luxurious stay while exploring the parks.

Budget-Friendly Hotels

1. Grant Village Lodge
- Price: $150-$250 per night
- Location: Yellowstone National Park, WY 82190
- Booking Contact: +1 307-344-7311

Grant Village Lodge offers affordable accommodations with basic amenities within Yellowstone National Park. The lodge is conveniently located near West Thumb Geyser Basin and Yellowstone Lake, making it an excellent choice for budget-conscious travelers seeking to experience the park's natural beauty.

2. Antler Inn

- Price: $100-$200 per night
- Location: 43 W Pearl Ave, Jackson, WY 83001
- Booking Contact: +1 307-733-2535

Antler Inn, located in downtown Jackson, provides comfortable and affordable lodging options. Guests can enjoy easy access to local shops, restaurants, and attractions. The hotel features cozy rooms, a fitness center, and a hot tub, making it a great value for those exploring both Yellowstone and Grand Teton National Parks.

3. Stagecoach Inn

- Price: $90-$180 per night
- Location: 209 Madison Ave, West Yellowstone, MT 59758
- Booking Contact: +1 406-646-7381

Stagecoach Inn, situated in West Yellowstone, offers budget-friendly accommodations with convenient access to the park's west entrance. The inn features comfortable rooms, an indoor pool, and a complimentary breakfast. Its location and amenities make it a popular choice for budget travelers.

Restaurants

1. The Lake House at Grand Teton Lodge Company
   - Location: 100 Jackson Lake Lodge Rd, Moran, WY 83013

The Lake House offers casual dining with stunning views of Jackson Lake and the Teton Range. Guests can enjoy a variety of American and regional dishes, including fresh trout and bison burgers, in a relaxed atmosphere.

2. Old Faithful Snow Lodge Obsidian Dining Room

- Location: 2051 Snow Lodge Ave, Yellowstone National Park, WY 82190

Located within the Old Faithful Snow Lodge, the Obsidian Dining Room provides a fine dining experience with a menu featuring locally sourced ingredients. The restaurant offers a range of options, from gourmet entrees to hearty comfort foods, all served in a cozy, lodge-style setting.

3. Local Restaurant and Bar
- Location: 55 N Cache St, Jackson, WY 83001

Local Restaurant and Bar is a popular spot in Jackson, known for its farm-to-table cuisine and vibrant atmosphere. The menu includes a variety of dishes, such as fresh seafood, prime steaks, and seasonal vegetables, highlighting the flavors of the region.

Chapter 11: Five-Day Itinerary

Day 1: Arrival & Exploration of Yellowstone National Park

Morning:

- Arrive at Yellowstone National Park through the North Entrance.
- Visit Mammoth Hot Springs to explore the terraced formations of travertine created by geothermal activity.
- Walk the boardwalks and take in the stunning views of the hot springs and surrounding landscape.

Afternoon:

- Drive to Norris Geyser Basin, one of the hottest and most dynamic geothermal areas in Yellowstone.
- Explore the Porcelain Basin and the Back Basin, marveling at the geysers, hot springs, and colorful thermal features.
- Stop for a picnic lunch at a designated area within the park.

Evening:
- Head to the Grand Canyon of Yellowstone.
- Enjoy the breathtaking views of the Lower and Upper Falls from various lookout points, such as Artist Point and Lookout Point.
- Return to your hotel for dinner and relaxation.

Day 2: Geysers and Hot Springs

Morning:

- Visit the iconic Old Faithful geyser in the Upper Geyser Basin.
- Witness an eruption of Old Faithful and explore the surrounding geothermal features, including the Morning Glory Pool and the Castle Geyser.

Afternoon:

- Travel to the Midway Geyser Basin to see the famous Grand Prismatic Spring.
- Walk the boardwalks and take in the vibrant colors of the largest hot spring in the United States.
- Have lunch at a nearby picnic area or one of the park's cafeterias.

Evening:

- Head to the West Thumb Geyser Basin along the shores of Yellowstone Lake.
- Explore the thermal features and enjoy the stunning views of the lake.

- Return to your hotel for dinner and relaxation.

Day 3: Wildlife Viewing and Scenic Drives

Morning:
- Start the day early with a visit to Lamar Valley, known for its abundant wildlife.
- Keep an eye out for bison, elk, wolves, and bears as you drive through the valley.
- Stop at pullouts and take short hikes to increase your chances of spotting wildlife.

Afternoon:
- Travel to Hayden Valley for more wildlife viewing opportunities.
- Enjoy a picnic lunch in the valley while observing the herds of bison and other animals.

- Continue to Yellowstone Lake for a scenic drive along the shoreline.

Evening:
- Visit the Fishing Bridge and take a leisurely walk along the Yellowstone River.
- Enjoy the peaceful ambiance and watch for waterfowl and other wildlife.
- Return to your hotel for dinner and relaxation.

Day 4: Grand Teton National Park Exploration

Morning:
- Depart for Grand Teton National Park via the John D. Rockefeller Jr. Memorial Parkway.
- Stop at the Colter Bay Visitor Center to gather information and plan your day.

- Take a scenic drive along Teton Park Road, stopping at various viewpoints for spectacular views of the Teton Range.

Afternoon:
- Visit Jenny Lake and take a boat shuttle across the lake.
- Hike the Hidden Falls and Inspiration Point trail for breathtaking views of the lake and mountains.
- Enjoy a picnic lunch by the lake.

Evening:
- Drive to the town of Jackson and explore the local shops and art galleries.
- Have dinner at one of Jackson's renowned restaurants.
- Return to your hotel for the night.

Day 5: Adventure and Departure

Morning:

- Start the day with a scenic float trip on the Snake River, offering stunning views of the Teton Range and opportunities to spot wildlife.
- Alternatively, choose a guided horseback ride through the park's trails.

Afternoon:

- Visit the Laurance S. Rockefeller Preserve and hike the easy trails through forests and meadows.
- Enjoy the tranquility and natural beauty of this lesser-known area of the park.
- Have lunch at a nearby picnic area or café.

Evening:

- Return to your hotel to pack and check out.
- Reflect on your adventures and make any last-minute stops in the park or town before departing for home.

Chapter 12: Tips for a Memorable Trip

Embarking on a journey to Yellowstone and Grand Teton National Parks promises unforgettable experiences amidst pristine landscapes, abundant wildlife, and cultural treasures. Whether you're a seasoned traveler or visiting for the first time, incorporating practical tips ensures a seamless and memorable adventure. From capturing stunning photographs and staying connected to preparing for emergencies, these insights enhance your journey while prioritizing safety, connectivity, and enjoyment.

Photography Tips

1. Equipment Essentials:
- Camera Gear: Pack a versatile camera with interchangeable lenses suitable for capturing

wide-angle landscapes, close-up wildlife shots, and detailed portraits. Consider a sturdy tripod for stability in low-light conditions or when photographing long exposures.

- Accessories: Carry spare batteries, memory cards with ample storage capacity, lens cleaning kits, and protective cases or bags to safeguard your equipment from dust, moisture, and impact.

2. Lighting and Timing:

- Golden Hours: Take advantage of soft, golden light during sunrise and sunset for atmospheric landscapes and silhouette photography. Consult sunrise and sunset times using mobile apps or park information to plan your shoots.
- Midday Challenges: Adjust camera settings and use polarizing filters to reduce glare and enhance colors when photographing midday scenes under harsh sunlight. Look for

shaded areas or cloud cover for more even lighting.

3. Composition Techniques:

- Rule of Thirds: Frame subjects off-center using the rule of thirds to create balanced compositions. Position horizons along the lower or upper third of the frame to emphasize sky or foreground elements.
- Leading Lines: Incorporate natural elements such as paths, rivers, or mountain ridges as leading lines guiding viewers' eyes through the photograph towards focal points or distant landscapes.

4. Wildlife Photography:

- Respectful Distance: Use telephoto lenses to capture detailed wildlife portraits from a safe distance, respecting animals' natural behaviors and minimizing disturbance. Avoid approaching or feeding wildlife for ethical and safety reasons.

- Patience and Observation: Remain patient and observant when photographing wildlife, anticipating movement or interactions that convey unique behaviors and moments in their natural habitats.

5. Landscapes and Reflections:

- Water Reflections: Capture mirror-like reflections of mountains, forests, and clouds in calm water surfaces such as lakes or ponds during early morning or late evening. Use a polarizing filter to enhance contrast and reduce reflections.
- Foreground Interest: Include foreground elements such as wildflowers, fallen trees, or rock formations to add depth and perspective to wide-angle landscape compositions.

6. Night Sky Photography:

- Astrophotography: Capture celestial phenomena including starscapes, Milky Way galaxies, and meteor showers in designated dark sky areas within the parks. Use long exposure techniques and adjust ISO settings for optimal clarity and detail.

- Light Painting: Experiment with light painting techniques using flashlights or headlamps to illuminate foreground objects against starry backgrounds, creating striking nocturnal compositions.

7. Editing and Post-Processing:

- RAW Format: Shoot in RAW format to retain maximum image quality and flexibility during post-processing adjustments. Use editing software to fine-tune exposure, contrast, color balance, and remove unwanted elements while preserving natural tones.

Staying Connected

1. Cellular Coverage and Wi-Fi Availability:

- Park Accessibility: Expect limited or no cellular reception in remote areas of Yellowstone and Grand Teton National Parks. Check with your mobile service provider regarding coverage maps and available network providers in nearby towns.

- Visitor Centers and Lodging: Access complimentary Wi-Fi services at visitor centers, lodges, and select campgrounds within the parks. Utilize these facilities for essential communications, weather updates, and online research.

2. Satellite Communication Devices:

- Emergency Preparedness: Consider renting or purchasing satellite phones or personal locator beacons (PLBs) for reliable communication in case of emergencies or when exploring remote backcountry areas with no cellular coverage.

- GPS Navigation: Use GPS-enabled devices or smartphone apps featuring offline maps and navigation tools to navigate trails, monitor route progress, and mark points of interest while conserving battery life.

3. Emergency Contact Information:
- Park Services: Familiarize yourself with emergency contact numbers for park rangers, medical services, and search and rescue operations available 24/7 within Yellowstone and Grand Teton National Parks.
- Family and Travel Contacts: Share your travel itinerary, lodging details, and emergency contact information with trusted family members, friends, or travel companions for added peace of mind during your trip.

4. Local Information Resources:

- Visitor Guides: Obtain comprehensive visitor guides, maps, and brochures from park visitor centers and information kiosks detailing park regulations, safety tips, and seasonal updates affecting visitor experiences.

- Weather Alerts: Monitor weather forecasts and severe weather alerts using NOAA Weather Radio, smartphone apps, or park information channels to stay informed about changing weather conditions and potential hazards.

5. Community Connectivity:

- Local Services: Engage with local communities and businesses in gateway towns such as Jackson, Wyoming, and West Yellowstone, Montana, offering additional resources, dining options, and recreational activities outside the parks.

- Cultural Experiences: Attend local events, festivals, and cultural programs showcasing regional heritage, arts, and traditions that complement your park visit and support community tourism initiatives.

What to Do in Case of Emergencies

1. Emergency Preparedness:

- Personal Safety: Prioritize personal safety and well-being by following park regulations, staying on designated trails, and avoiding risky behaviors such as feeding wildlife or approaching geothermal features.

- First Aid Kit: Carry a well-equipped first aid kit containing essential supplies for treating minor injuries, cuts, insect bites, and illnesses encountered during outdoor activities in remote park locations.

2. Communication and Alert Systems:

- Park Alerts: Stay informed about park closures, trail advisories, and emergency alerts issued by park rangers or visitor centers through public address systems, signage, and digital message boards.
- Emergency Notifications: Register for emergency notification services provided by park management, including text message alerts or automated phone calls regarding safety advisories and evacuation procedures.

3. Search and Rescue Protocols:
- Reporting Emergencies: Immediately report emergencies, accidents, or lost individuals to park rangers or emergency services by dialing 911 or using emergency call boxes located at designated trailheads and visitor facilities.
- Search Procedures: Provide detailed information about your location, physical description, and medical conditions to aid search and rescue efforts conducted by

trained personnel equipped with specialized equipment and resources.

4. *Wildlife Encounters:*

- Safety Guidelines: Maintain a safe distance from wildlife species such as bison, elk, and bears encountered in their natural habitats. Use binoculars or telephoto lenses for observation and avoid disturbing animals by approaching or feeding them.
- Bear Safety: Familiarize yourself with bear safety protocols, including carrying bear spray, traveling in groups, and properly storing food and scented items in bear-resistant containers or designated storage lockers.

5. *Travel Insurance and Documentation:*

- Policy Coverage: Review travel insurance policies to verify coverage for medical emergencies, evacuation services, and trip cancellations or interruptions occurring within national park boundaries.

- Document Management: Keep copies of essential travel documents, including passports, driver's licenses, health insurance cards, and emergency contact information stored securely in waterproof containers or digital formats accessible offline.

6. Community Support and Assistance:

- Visitor Assistance: Seek assistance from park rangers, visitor center staff, or fellow visitors in case of emergencies requiring immediate medical attention, transportation assistance, or communication with emergency services.

- Community Outreach: Engage with local communities, nonprofit organizations, and emergency response agencies supporting visitor safety initiatives and promoting responsible outdoor recreation practices within Yellowstone and Grand Teton National Parks.

By integrating photography techniques, staying connected through reliable communication channels, and preparing for emergencies with proactive measures and community support, you enhance the safety, enjoyment, and overall experience of your journey through Yellowstone and Grand Teton National Parks. Embrace the natural beauty, cultural heritage, and outdoor adventures while preserving these treasured landscapes for future generations to explore and appreciate.